Heritage of Hope

Lives Touched by God's Transforming Power

Jan Edith Taylor

InspiringVoices®
A Service of **Guideposts**

Inspiring Voices books may be ordered through booksellers or by contacting:

Inspiring Voices
1663 Liberty Drive
Bloomington, IN 47403
www.inspiringvoices.com
1-(866) 697-5313

Because of the dynamic nature of the Internet, any web addresses or links contained in this book may have changed since publication and may no longer be valid. The views expressed in this work are solely those of the author and do not necessarily reflect the views of the publisher, and the publisher hereby disclaims any responsibility for them.

Any people depicted in stock imagery provided by Thinkstock are models, and such images are being used for illustrative purposes only.

Certain stock imagery © Thinkstock.

ISBN: 978-1-4624-0459-9 (sc)
ISBN: 978-1-4624-0460-5 (e)

Library of Congress Control Number: 2012922689

Printed in the United States of America

Inspiring Voices rev. date: 01/22/2013

Contents

To all the story-tellers in every culture, and the children and children's children who benefit from hearing about the wondrous works of God.

Acknowledgements

When I began this project roughly six years ago, there was so much I had to learn about publishing. It took me awhile to actually accept the fact that God would entrust these wonderful stories to me. All along the way the Holy Spirit gave me confidence and guidance, supplying just the person and expertise I needed at every juncture. This is a book He chose to publish and I give Him glory and praise for His grace all along the way.

First of all, appreciation to Eddie, my companion of 50 years and my encourager in this project. He has always believed that I was meant to be a writer, even when I had trouble believing it myself.

Thank you to CLASServices Writers Conference in New Mexico and the Publish It Now! Workshops who mentored this first-time author twice in three years and published two of my stories. What an inspiring place to have begun my writing task! Thank you, Linda Gilden, Editorial Director and organizer of the workshops, and all the CLASS leadership, fellow writers, editors, publishers, speakers, and worshipers who shared their visions with us, the beginners.

Kudos to my local Irish Hills Writers Group, especially Tom Boyer, Bonnie McJennett, Terry Mahr, and Pat Grau who faithfully critiqued my writing over a period of years. Thank you, Margaret Cantrell, my exchange friend from ICYE when we were seventeen, who entered my life again in 1988, and became editor for this project these last several years. I must also mention Bronwyn Barricklow, a busy elementary school teacher and neighbor who has such wonderful creative gifts. She and I connect in a way only God could orchestrate.

Bronwyn helped me with titles and to organize ideas when I was off on several tangents at once.

Finally, I owe a great debt of gratitude to the story-tellers who have waited patiently for their stories to finally be published. Thank you for your lives lived in obedience to God and for His Face that shines forth in your encounters with Him. Thank you for your faithfulness in wanting to get your stories out to the public and share them with your families, your grandchildren and the next generation so that "they might set their hope in God, and not forget the works of God." (Psalm 78: 7 – NRSV)

Jan Edith Taylor

Introduction

Sitting next to my desk on a wrought iron table with sculpted grape leaves, sits an Israeli plate with a vivid mosaic design: electric blues, rich corals, and deep greens. On the plate I have placed a mound of rough, natural stones, each stone selected to represent a gracious work of God in my life. When I look at the small memorial, I feel peace. God is faithful; He has brought me through many struggles. In 1 Peter 2:4b, 5, 9 (NRSV) the apostle says "Come to him, a living stone…and like living stones…let yourselves be built into a spiritual house, …But you are a chosen race, a royal priesthood, a holy nation, God's own people, in order that you may proclaim the mighty acts of him who called you out of darkness into his marvelous light." Psalm 87:4 (NRSV) instructs God's people to relate the stories of the faith to our children. "We will tell to the coming generation the glorious deeds of the Lord, and his might, and the wonders that he has done."

At my first Writers Conference, sponsored by CLASS, an established writer and publisher walked with me to the dining hall one morning, and hearing about the stories I was collecting, he told me that everyone was writing stories like these. "If you want to be published," he counseled me, "you need to have a niche." At that time several books about the faith of military families had come on the market and they were selling well. I stored this advice in the back of my mind, as a nagging thought that somehow did not fit my book at all. The people in my stories came from a variety of careers, a number of Christian denominations, and some of the encounters with God were gentle leadings while others were vividly supernatural. How would I find a platform to market a book with such an amalgamation?

A few days after I returned home, I was watching the evening news. Overwhelmingly the accounts presented individuals in dire circumstances, seemingly without hope. The Holy Spirit brought to my mind the comment from the writers' conference and I sensed God saying, "You see the stories of tragic events in people's lives every day in the media, but there is no hope because they avoid mentioning My redeeming power. Your mentor was correct. There are many people recounting stories such as the ones you are seeking to publish, and that is because I am *calling* many people to tell the whole truth: There is a God Who cares and Who helps those who call upon His supernatural power in their need."

God has a way of reaching each of us when He has a message He wants to relay. Reading Psalm 78 one morning, the Holy Spirit impressed on my mind that I was, indeed, to pass on stories I was hearing from people's encounters with God. I put off the call for several months thinking, "Why would God choose me—an untried, unpolished writer—when there are writers who are already established and polished in their craft as writers—and He could have anyone He wanted?" Yet, over and over, I could be most anywhere and before I knew it, someone would begin to tell me the most tender, supernaturally-charged story.

After several months of entertaining insecurities I prayed, "Okay, Lord, I am getting the message, but where should I start?" The impression was, "Start with your mother." That morning I was to go visit my mother about an hour away. A woman of great wisdom and common sense, then in her nineties, she was facing decisions about going into assisted living. I knew the schedule would be super-charged with issues she would need to discuss, but nevertheless, I put a yellow pad under my arm as I was leaving.

As I expected, the morning passed and there never seemed to be a moment that was "right" for me to present the idea of writing her story. As I was preparing to leave, I broached the subject of my project, and of the impression I thought God had given me that I was to have hers be the first story. "I know this is not a good time to talk much about this, but I brought some paper and if you would jot down a few notes as something comes to mind, we can discuss it at a better time," I graciously offered.

Mom looked at me askance and said, "I already have it written!" And she did! At a women's retreat in the 1980's mom had given her testimony and she retrieved it from her file and handed it over to me. I had my first story!

Dear Reader, it has taken me six years to finish this project, and during this time I have read and re-read these stories many times, and they have never ceased to inspire me. My prayer is that they will enrich your lives as well, and that in them, God's love for you will be stirred and renewed.

To Him be all glory, honor, and praise – the God above all gods. Amen.

Jan Edith Taylor

SUPERNATURAL CALL

Rev. Dr. James Boos

Plumber and pipe fitter Jim Boos felt the heat of the sun on his back that clear day in March 1963. The sensation was pleasant after another harsh Ohio winter, but the sight before him was anything but pleasant. Deep in muddy trenches, his crew was on their knees laying pipe for the junior high in Lauren, Ohio. The spring thaw was melting the frost and Jim could see the banks of these ditches had become soft and treacherous. At any moment there could be a cave-in. He told the men to clean their tools and head for home. Conditions were too perilous to continue the work.

After assuring himself that everything was in order at the construction site, Jim climbed into his car and began the 45 minute drive home.

He was feeling good. The project at the junior high was going well and the day was beautiful—clear blue skies, not a cloud to be seen. Yet in his spirit he was vaguely conscious of a *prompting*. While he resisted naming the question, all he could think to say was, "No." As he drove the familiar highway, he spoke the resistant word aloud, "No." And then again, "no." And for thirty minutes the only word that rose from within was again, "no."

"Am I going crazy?" he wondered. He pulled his car into the driveway leading to the family farm where he and his wife and children had an apartment. Slowly he got out of the car, and began to walk toward the farmhouse, but the urging did not let up. Jim stopped and looked up into the beautiful expanse of the heavens.

"Father," he prayed aloud, "I do not wish to show you any disrespect, but if you want me to go into the ministry, then you will have to show me more than indigestion." He paused a moment and a thought came across his mind, and he prayed it aloud, "Father, in the Old Testament you indicated your will for man through natural occurrences" ...then shrugging his shoulders he said, *"like lightning."*

"Wham! Kaboom! Instantly out of the serenity of the spring sky a bolt of lightning struck in the midst of four trees about ten to twelve feet away. The force of natural energy carved a path about a foot across and sprayed stones over the amazed contractor.

Jim was not startled. He was not frightened. *Jim was elated.* As he bounded up the stairs leading to the apartment, his wife met him at the door. She was wondering what had caused an explosion in the tranquility of the quiet afternoon. Jim quickly told her of his prayer and what he had witnessed. The couple knelt on the floor and prayed, "Father, we will follow wherever you lead us. We will walk off a plank into outer darkness if you tell us to."

Conscious that an exciting adventure was opening before him, Jim called his pastor and asked for an appointment, "as soon as possible." The minister agreed to meet Jim in his office at 7:30 that evening. As Jim quietly and with conviction told him what had happened, the blood drained from the face of the pastor. Then, vehemently he told Jim, *"You must forget this ever happened."* Jim was speechless.

The minister continued in an outburst of fury, "This is a coincidence... you need to forget it. You are a plumber... you are much better off as a plumber. You make good money as a plumber. Why would you want to do anything else?"

The demeaning remarks continued to batter away at Jim's confidence. "Do you have any idea how difficult and demanding seminary is? I know you and you'll never make it through." Drawing a breath, "How would you support your family?"

Further, with an attempt at rationalization, "Jim, you are an elder, a leader in the church; you serve on the Session. That is enough. You need to forget this ever happened!"

Jim left the church in confusion. What had he done to provoke such an angry reaction? His pastor's diatribe left him feeling demoralized and yes... spiritually unclean. As he headed home he wondered, "Am I in the wrong denomination? What should I do with this wonderful calling?"

Firm in their belief that God had, indeed, called Jim to the ministry, the Boos family packed their things, said goodbye to the home place, and headed to Columbus, Ohio.

At Ohio State University Jim pursued a B.S. degree in education. He had a family to support, the expense of seeking higher education, and he was starting from scratch—his 57 credit hours in engineering useless in his new career direction. The challenges were daunting.

The confirmation of his call, which he had hoped to hear from his minister, now came through an unlikely friendship at Springfield Roller Company where Jim was hired as a welder. He worked the night shift attending class by day. Because of the masks welders wear men did not have much opportunity to socialize with one another. But Jim noticed one man in particular seemed bent on keeping himself separate from the rest. Big John was six feet four inches tall with a forbidding countenance. When suppertime arrived, the man sought the isolation of a corner where a street light cast faint illumination though a window covered by dust from the men's welding and grinding. There Big John sat on the concrete floor in a powder so deep one could write his name. Leaning against the wall, he ate silently and alone.

Something about the man's loneliness drew Jim. One evening he risked approaching Big John. "Do you mind if I eat with you?" he asked the imposing man.

Big John looked up and mumbled, "It's a free country. Pull up a piece of cement and have a seat."

Simple conversation about their work and the challenges of the job, led to a comfortable camaraderie and the two men began to eat together on a regular basis. Then one night, Big John turned toward Jim and began to tell his story.

During World War II John was a frogman who operated in secrecy behind Japanese lines. A submarine would drop him off in a cove for a maneuver lasting thirty days. In a raft and a rubber suit, armed only with a knife and a 45 pistol, this man would paddle quietly to an island occupied by the enemy and under cover of night, would bury his raft, suit, and pistol. Then, knife in hand, he began moving among the trees, gathering information about the strength of the Japanese troops and equipment. Forced to remain on alert by his subversive assignment for those thirty days, he rarely slept. If anyone discovered his presence he was trained to silence that person, instructed as he was in eighteen different ways to kill with his bare hands in a manner of seconds.

At the end of the assignment John would depart as silently as he had come. Uncovering his raft, he paddled to a designated spot where again the submarine would surface at a specific time. The vessel would wait only 45 minutes to reconnoiter with the soldier. If he did *not* make contact within that period of time, John was told the submarine would leave and it would not return.

John was effective in his mission, and returned home safely to his family. However, it was soon apparent that he would never again be able to return to his tranquil life of before the War. His emotions, tightly strung from sleepless nights and days behind Japanese lines, refused to heal even after extensive training to clear his mind. At night his wife would rock him, his head in her lap, while he cried out from the nightmarish visions that arose from his subconscious. She locked the door of their bedroom, in fear that some commotion during the night would trigger his training and endanger their children.

Finally, agonizing over his dangerous responses to the daily routines within his household, John made the decision to live alone. He welded nights and visited his family during the day. He chose to isolate himself from people, fearing that in some angry outburst he might kill someone before he even knew what he was doing.

Jim was touched and awed by the man's story. Uncertain how to respond, Jim's eyes communicated his feelings of compassion to his companion. "How could he ease the man's suffering?" he thought to himself.

Then, John looked at his newfound friend intently and asked, "What is *your* story?"

Jim hesitated a moment. Since the evening in his pastor's study, he had never shared the details of his call with anyone. Now he told Big John of the unusual answer to his prayer for guidance that day on the farm. Through the semi-darkness of the weld shop Jim could see tears well up in Big John's eyes. *He began to sob* as Jim told him how the direction of his life had changed after the lightning strike. When the story was finished, Big John looked straight into his friend's face and said, "Thank you, Jim, for sharing your call. Now I *know* ...there *is* a God."

Jim says about God's supernatural call to the pastorate: "Down through the years I have learned that I have to be very careful in sharing this call. Some people are not ready to hear it. Some are shaken by a spiritual happening that stretches them. But there are others who embrace this story with tears of understanding and thankfulness." *Like Big John.*

A NIGHT OF TENSION IN VIET NAM

Jon D. Strother, Maj. USAF (Ret.)

The heat and humidity of the Viet Nam evening pressed in on the young captain as he strode toward the Quonset hut on the massive Tan Son Nhut Air Base, just outside Saigon.

It was the early 1970's. American protests against involvement in the war in Viet Nam were front-page news, something that discouraged the soldiers who every day confronted the enemy.

Jon Strother was the senior intelligence officer assigned to the 377th Air Base Wing. One of the few black officers on base, Jon knew that he had earned the respect of his commanding officer, Colonel David O'Dell. A man old enough to be Jon's father, the Colonel was energetic but demanding. In Jon's opinion, his commanding officer was smart, fair, and not a racist.

Word had spread that evening that a potentially volatile meeting of black enlisted men was to take place. So Jon was not surprised when he was summoned to Colonel O'Dell's office and instructed to attend the gathering and assume the sensitive role of observer.

Interaction among races in the military in the 1970s reflected racial tensions in the United States. But on assignment in Viet Nam all American servicemen worked together to accomplish their missions. The barracks and the mess hall on base were common meeting areas but upon entering these buildings, one immediately noticed that soldiers voluntarily separated themselves into racial groups. In recognition of this, a Quonset hut had been designated to give black enlisted men a place to hang out and engage in recreational activities. Everyone on base was aware of this facility—and some resented its existence.

One night, under the cover of darkness, someone burned a cross in front of the Quonset hut, sending a fiery message of hate and intimidation. Passions were ignited by this event lending an underlying threat of violence on a military base where weapons were readily available. To make matters worse, no one, including the security guard whose post gave him line-of-sight to the burning cross, claimed any knowledge regarding the perpetrator. The burning of the cross intensified already raw feelings among African Americans who frequented the facility. They decided to organize to find and punish the person who burned the cross.

A meeting was called and perhaps as many as seventy-five black troops assembled one evening to decide what to do and how to gain justice in this matter. The general feeling was that the official investigation was moving too slowly and the black troops presumed there would be a cover-up.

In fact, Colonel O'Dell had initiated an investigation immediately upon learning of the incident. The local Air Force Office of Special Investigations had begun an inquiry that had already identified a suspect. However, the collection of evidence was not complete and an arrest was still pending.

Meanwhile, Jon was assigned to observe the meeting and report the results to Colonel O'Dell. Jon's loyalty to the uniform he wore was unwavering. Nevertheless, in his role as observer he did not want to be seen as a spy who would betray his racial counterparts. Certainly, it would require wisdom to balance his responsibilities with his loyalties to the men.

As Jon entered the recreation building, the men acknowledged the presence of an officer. Accustomed to greeting one another with a special handshake called a "Dap," black enlisted men would not give an officer this greeting. Nevertheless, when they saluted their racial counterpart outside, they gave the snappy gesture an extra flourish. The creative movement included him as one of the "brothers" while respecting his rank.

Jon took an unobtrusive position at the back of the room noticing that, although there were metal folding chairs and tables, most of those attending chose to stand, a sure sign of their level of agitation. Word had spread rapidly of the topic of the assembly and many of the enlisted men were concerned about what the outcome might be. The soldiers chatted quietly in groups, eyes scanning the gathering crowd to assess who was there.

As the meeting began, a very eloquent but angry young enlisted man assumed the leadership role. He voiced his anger over the cross burning incident, his impatience with the pace of the investigation, and his distrust of "the system." He proposed his own solutions to the problem and encouraged others to support and join in his proposed actions. Several of the individuals at the meeting voiced their agreement with the young man, while others offered a more cautious approach.

The meeting lasted the better part of an hour.

Toward the end of the discussion, the young leader noted Jon's presence and invited him to voice his opinion about what had happened and his impressions of their meeting. Jon's instructions were to observe, but he felt that he must speak. He had a responsibility as an officer to act as leader and *this was a time to lead*. He had the respect of most of the black troops on the base but if he lost it, he would never be credible with these men in the future.

Jon hesitated. He had no idea what he would say. The room became silent and all eyes were on the young captain. Jon bought some time by walking slowly and deliberately to the front of the room. He recognized that if this group followed their leader's course, there could be a serious racial incident on the base, potentially resulting in unnecessary injuries and perhaps even death to our own troops. "We Americans do not need to be fighting ourselves," the officer thought silently to himself.

Jon decided to direct his comments to the leader and his supporters who were grouped to his right. These men clearly exercised influence over the enlisted men in the room.

Rather than challenging or lecturing them, Jon began with a series of questions. The success of his strategy was dependent upon the leader's willingness to respond as Jon hoped he would. Jon asked the men to put themselves in the position of the commander and consider his responsibility to maintain order on his base. Jon's queries brought into bold relief the potential risks to those who participated in vigilante activities, and how this would play in the news back home. Jon listened in wonder as the leader and his supporters moved, via their replies, to argue logically with themselves and their proposed actions. The men's responses acknowledged possible and probable outcomes of the actions they proposed to take. This must have gone on for fifteen or twenty minutes. By the end of the dialogue, a majority of the group was unwilling to follow their leader and was ready to permit the official process to take its course.

When it was over, several of the men shook Jon's hand or patted him on the back as they left the building. Despite the apparent success, he overheard one of the men from the leader's band state that he knew who had burned the cross. *He vowed he would make sure that person paid for his act.*

Jon advised Col. O'Dell to have the man suspected of burning the cross placed in protective custody in order to avoid any retributive action by anyone attending the meeting. Col. O'Dell acted swiftly and the suspect was flown out of Viet Nam to Hawaii where, Jon was told, he was subjected to disciplinary action.

During the following thirty plus years, Jon has often thought about how close that perpetrator—he never knew his name—came to suffering some grave consequences and how near the base came to having a serious racial incident. When the opportunity came to speak at the meeting, Jon confesses he felt like Moses. "Why me?" he asked himself. Up to that time, Jon had never been a very good public speaker, without thoroughly preparing in advance.

He attributes his success to what one might call "divine intervention," because he has no clue, based on his experience and training up to that time, how he did what he did that night.

GRAMEMA'S STORY

Joan Thomas

"I will be alright." The words lingered in the air.

My pregnant daughter-in-law, Mary, and I listened intently as my son Tyler shared a dream from the night before. In his dream he saw a hospital room, all in white, where a group of doctors hovered over a baby on a surgical table. Their hands were on the infant's heart as though they were resuscitating the baby. The child's head, which seemed unusually large and mature, suddenly turned toward my son and said, "*I will be alright*." While Tyler seemed concerned with the message of the dream, Mary and I passed it off as a result of his caring nature. "Everything will be fine," we reassured him.

At five months Mary's appointment for her ultrasound went well, and so we celebrated that afternoon by shopping for baby furniture. However, a week later the doctor called with devastating news. The ultrasound revealed there was a severe problem with the baby's heart. If the child survived to full term, it could not live long thereafter, he advised. To avoid heartache, he suggested the parents consider an abortion. Mary answered immediately with quiet conviction, "*No...* We will not consider an abortion."

When Mary told me the news, her words between sobs were almost unintelligible. We cried together, and then we began to pray. We tried to make sense of it all. "God will get us through," we told each other. Then, as Mary read in her Bible the story of Abraham's sacrifice of Isaac on the altar, she relinquished her pregnancy and the baby to the Lord.

The next days and weeks were filled with ups and downs. At Mott Children's Hospital in Ann Arbor, Michigan, the expectant parents were interviewed by psychologists, heart specialists, and others on the hospital staff. In the midst of uncertainty, we recalled my son's dream, and realized it was a gift to comfort us. It helped us believe that Our Heavenly Father was present in all of this—there was a plan—God was in control. Each time there seemed to be no hope, we would remember the words, "I will be alright," and considered that no matter if the baby lived with us or with the Lord in heaven, indeed he would be alright; he was in God's hands. For the rest of us, as we walked by faith, depending on the Holy Spirit to lead us, our perspective changed. We were excited to watch God at work.

Details began to emerge: the baby was a boy and his problem was Hypo-plastic Left Heart Syndrome. In this abnormality the left side of the heart is small and unable to pump enough blood to meet the body's needs. Doctors told the parents of a new procedure that might correct the problem, but it had only been done fifteen times and then in a hospital in Boston. Tyler and Mary turned to God and prayed for guidance, and the answer impressed on their minds, was, "Yes. Go."

Before they left for Boston, Mary's mom put together a baby shower. It was a joyous time. We were all aware of the need to stay positive, and to rely on God. After Mary had opened the many wonderful gifts, we surrounded her, making a circle, our arms around each other while we prayed for God's blessing. We were at peace. All the bases were covered. The expectant parents flew to Boston with no time to waste!

When the plane landed at Logan Airport, Mary and Tyler decided to name this baby, about whom there was such confident trust, Logan Emanuel (God is with us) Thomas.

The inter-uterine surgery began after Mary had been sedated with the hope that the anesthetic would also keep Logan calm. After three hours in which the team of surgeons tried every procedure to repair the problem, his tiny heart stopped beating. Cardiologists had considered this risk, warning that no baby's heart had ever recovered once it stopped. As they feverishly massaged Logan's heart, miraculously it recovered. God was with them! However, with great disappointment the doctors discovered that Logan was not calm enough for them to continue to operate.

Returning home, Mary and Tyler chose to believe that God was still in control. Nevertheless, how would they pay for the expensive yet unsuccessful surgery in Boston? In prayer together and leaning on God, they saw Him move. All bills were taken care of, including the flight to Boston. God's angels here on earth stepped forward to help.

Now, new choices were presented and decisions must be made. Should they seek a heart transplant or a three part surgery known as the Norwood Procedure? The Norwood Procedure would reconstruct the baby's heart. And what if the doctors' predictions came true and the baby did not survive his birth? Should they also prepare for his death?

The Norwood Procedure began to look like the best option. The first operation would be at birth, another at six months, and the final reconstructive surgery at eighteen months. After much prayer, the parents stated: "This baby's heart is the one God gave him, and we will put our reliance on God. He will work through the doctors, to do the three-part surgery."

During this time I struggled in prayer, taking authority, commanding in Jesus' name that all negative doubts and fears leave my mind. In the quiet that followed, "God is with us," and the words of the baby in my son's dream. It also helped to visualize a little infant boy sleeping in his baby bed, wearing the beautiful clothes from the shower. That became my focus: to have that picture of *life*; to praise God and to remember churches, friends, and relatives were praying earnestly for this little one. It amazed me that so many people were willing to be involved and totally committed to saving the life of this unborn child. It reminded me of the love God places in our hearts for Himself, even though we have not seen Him. I would tell myself: *Logan is alive—act like he is.*

On August 19, 2003, Logan's due date, Mary went to the hospital to have the birth induced. After much effort on the part of the medical staff and this faithful mother, Logan was born naturally, weighing almost nine pounds, crying and breathing on his own. His parents could hold him for a short time, then off to Holden Babies Intensive Care Unit for the next three days. I could only praise God and marvel at how beautiful Logan was!

Then on day three it was off to surgery.

Early on the day of his procedure I came to be with Logan. I placed my hand on his head and with the other cradled his feet and sang and prayed over him. Meanwhile, Logan would rest his right hand on his heart—not a cry—his chest rising higher on the right side, his breathing not quite normal. This first little grandson—how I loved him!

The wait after the surgery seemed interminable but finally we heard the news: Logan had sailed through the first operation. The specialist told us, with a look of wonder, that every so often there is a child whose body, throughout the surgery and the healing process, responds to everything in an optimum manner. "I call these children 'stars,' and Logan is one of those," he told us. Our prayers had been answered!

Now it was time to wait and let healing take place. The doctors called this period between the first and the second surgery the "honeymoon period." There were plugs, monitors, and feeding tubes on baby Logan. Mom pumped breast milk to mix with a special formula. So much was expected of Mary.

Tyler and Mary met other parents going through the same ordeal. Nurses would comment on Mary and Tyler's strength and even ask their help to console or give hope and comfort to others. Sometimes the request was just that they pray.

The day finally came when Logan could go home. The first eighteen months the baby would be in quarantine but the family of three tried to be as normal as possible. The parents found a church where they could sing praises to God for the miracles that had taken place. Both Mary and Tyler were baptized as a sign of their renewed faith in Jesus Christ.

In their church they joined a small circle of believers who dedicated themselves to pray for this little one. These Christians became a lifeline of support to the young parents. Meanwhile, each Sunday I would go to my church and then while I babysat with Logan, his parents would go to a later service at their church. Classes in CPR gave my husband and me confidence to care for Logan, and again we prayed we would make the right choices as we cared for this fragile little boy.

Logan was six months old when he had his second surgery, and as with the first, he did so well that in two weeks he was home. Now there were new challenges. To hear his voice was beautiful, but we always had to be careful not to let him cry too hard. We had to watch that he not become too hot or too cold; his abnormal coloring was evidence that his circulation system needed to improve. No one with a cold or the flu could come near him.

Nevertheless, we were astounded at how normally he progressed. He was smart; the morphine and the trauma of those first months of his life did not slow his development—he walked at twelve months, began to talk at fourteen months.

His parents, as well, were returning to normal life. Just two months before Logan was scheduled for the third surgery, Mary gave birth to Logan's brother, Kalen Jacob.

Logan responded well to his third operation, but more daily prayer was needed. Mom or Dad had to stay at the hospital continuously, and for four weeks the grandparents took care of baby Kalen. This was a time of added strain. Dad had to go to work. Logan could talk now, and he said things it pained his parents to hear: he did not like the medicine he was taking; he began to lose trust in his mother and the nurses because they insisted he take that awful stuff; and he suffered from the tubes in his neck and everywhere. Meanwhile, his grandparents brought his brother, Kalen, to the hospital every day so that Mom and Dad could hold their new baby and feed him.

Finally the day came when Logan could get out of bed. He loved playing in a sandbox at the hospital. Like any other preschooler, he constantly wanted visitors to read to him, especially me, his "Gramema."

Logan is now six years old. His lungs and his heart are strong. He takes just half a baby aspirin and one heart pill per day. He attends school and is very active. We praise the Lord that through Christ all things are possible. (Philippians 4:13)

As I look back on the decisions made about my grandson's life, and the way God guided us at every turn, I think to myself, *The Lord sets the stage and when we ask for Him to be our director, we are so rewarded!* Each child that comes into this world is God's, on loan to us to care for and nurture and to teach about His Son, Jesus Christ. God's presence in my life has been revealed to me in so many ways, so many times, that I have no doubt of His power, His wisdom, and His love. Thank you, God. Thank You, Jesus.

"THE DISCOVERY OF PEACE"

Reatha Meyer

Christmas Eve of 1971 I was caught up in the same frenzied pace of holidays in the past. I put myself in the position of being responsible for my family to have a perfect Christmas. Each one should receive the gifts that were currently at the top of their list and some that were the product of my own imagination. I incorporated into this season all the special traditions from my family plus those considered a must from my husband's side. Finally, each year we added new traditions for our young children.

My check list required that for months I spend all my days, and many nights too, accomplishing all the necessary chores. I thought they were important, and no one could have persuaded me they would not make my loved ones happy. I was convinced that to be a proper wife and mother these duties were part of my job. I now know it was to fulfill my own needs: I thought if I could achieve the perfect Christmas, my family would surely love and appreciate me more.

That year, I realized this holiday would be no different from the ones before. I could see the same pattern of behavior on my part and also in members of my family. The children were in an exceptionally high state of expectation about the holiday. I still had many things to do to prepare for the next morning's "dance about the Christmas Tree." The house had to be clean, uncluttered, beautifully decorated, every room of the house full of holiday cheer. I pleaded with the children to help me get ready. "Do your part!" But, in their excitement they could not concentrate on helping but only hindered my progress. I was exhausted, frustrated, and agitated with three excited children and a husband attempting to assure me I had done enough, but I could not hear.

Finally, I broke under the strain, provoked an argument, grabbed my coat and keys, and went for a ride alone. I didn't go far but drove through the city streets feeling alone, rejected, unloved and certainly unappreciated. I had spent months preparing so that my family would have a superior celebration, and they all sat back and refused to do their part to make my Christmas happy.

As I drove through the decorated streets, I treated myself to a royal pity party. I was so angry and hurt that I yelled out loud, "God, where is all this peace on earth that everyone is singing about?" No one had worked more earnestly than I had, and it did not make sense to me. This "peace on earth, goodwill to men" had totally eluded me again this year. I wanted to run away from my ungrateful family.

At last, like so many times before, I made a decision to just go back and try harder. After all, they were my family. I had to finish the commitment I had made. There was no quitting. Besides, where could I run to? There was no place that I would rather be than with my family in our home.

Then in January with all the Christmas trappings packed away and the children back in school except for the youngest, I settled down to endure the rest of winter. As Lent approached, our pastor made some simple suggestions to prepare for Easter. I decided to take time daily to read something of a spiritual nature. I was not an eager reader, but each day I would give my four year old son his lunch, tuck him into bed for a nap, and use that quiet time to read some old issues of Catholic Digest. It never occurred to me, at the time, to read the scriptures. I did not enjoy reading the Bible because it was difficult to understand. As the weeks of Lent progressed, I was committed to this time of spiritual reading.

Meanwhile, I had been actively involved in our parish as a Sunday school coordinator and Mother-Teacher of the preschool program. I had been teaching while my two older children were enrolled and now continued with the youngest. It involved a great amount of time and effort but I loved it and derived personal satisfaction from the preparation. I probably worked harder because I felt inadequate and lacked confidence. Studying for the lessons was a time of real grace for me. In order to teach these young children I needed to first know and love God the way a child of four or five could know and love Him, and that is what I began to experience. Week after week there was no doubt in my mind that I was getting more out of these classes than the children; yet I did hope it was benefiting them too.

On Holy Thursday I attended a charismatic Mass at the I.H.M. (Sisters of the Immaculate Heart of Mary) motherhouse at the invitation of another preschool teacher. She gave me no introduction to this charismatic Mass. In no way did she prepare me for what I was to observe and experience that night.

Chairs were set up in a basement meeting room with a portable altar. Guitar music began as the priest, robed in vestments, entered the room. Approximately 100 people were assembled. I was shocked when the Mass began and people leapt to their feet and began shouting prayers of praise and thanksgiving. I had never heard nor seen this done before.

My initial thought was "Why, these people have got to be a bunch of phonies. No one prays like that!" Immediately another thought followed, "except the saints."

"Where did that thought come from?" I wondered. "Yes, perhaps the saints in heaven would pray like that," I reasoned. Then another thought, "Remember the lesson you taught the children about how God calls all of us to be saints?" That evening when similar doubts arose, they were quickly dispelled.

The woman who had invited me suggested that we go into the Special Intentions Room for intercessory prayer. People formed a large circle and as each request was mentioned, someone would pray extemporaneously for that request. Not one rote prayer was said. Rote prayers were the only prayers I knew so I kept quiet, holding the hand of the person on each side.

I was reacting with one wave of goose bumps after another. This entire evening had been packed with new experiences. It made me giddy. The other women who knew me took delight in my smiling demeanor because they had never seen me this way. Later, as I recalled their reaction, I realized how serious and tense I must normally have seemed. They had never seen me laugh like this.

Before I left the motherhouse that evening two people gave me some specific instructions. One handed me a book called Catholic Pentecostals and another person told me to read the Acts of the Apostles in the Bible.

The next day I picked up a little paperback New Testament a friend had given me and for three days I read constantly, alternating with the Acts of the Apostles and the book, Catholic Pentecostals. I read and re-read and marveled at what I was learning. "This is too good to be true," I thought to myself.

I recall talking on the phone to the friend who had invited me to the Mass, telling her how I had been reading. "Praise God, these things are really wonderful," I told her enthusiastically. Yet the more I read the more questions I had. At one point I felt the presence of God all around me. In that moment some things became clear to me: God knew I existed; He knew me personally and He loved me even with all my faults and weaknesses. I was filled with warmth and love. The scriptures were no longer difficult to understand. When I went outside there was a new awareness in everything I saw. The sun was brighter; the air was fresher, crisper, and so exhilarating. I felt lightened from fears, worries, and doubts; there was a sense of new hope. I was experiencing the "peace on earth" I sought on Christmas Eve. I saw and felt and heard God in everything.

I returned for prayer meetings every Thursday night for about three years. They were the high point of my week. Some very close friendships were made during that time. Even today, although I may not have seen my friends for a long time, when we meet we begin to share and enjoy one another as though we have never been apart.

Once, as I was talking with some of the ladies after a prayer meeting, I learned the experience I was having is called the Baptism in the Holy Spirit. They explained that often this revelation comes to people as they ask others to lay hands on them and to pray for the filling of the Holy Spirit. This new life was so wonderful I never wanted to lose it. I never wanted to go back to the old life again. When Jesus said He came to give us life and give it more abundantly (John 10:10 - RSV), I understood that now in my own experience. What a comfort it was to learn God promised he would never leave me or forsake me (Hebrews 13:5 - RSV).

One evening about two months later, I turned on the television and caught the last five to ten minutes of a Billy Graham Crusade. I had seen one of his movies a few years before and recalled how I wanted to go forward at the invitation to make a commitment to Jesus Christ. At the time fear held me back from doing so. But this time, when I heard Billy give the invitation to surrender to the Lordship of Jesus Christ, I knew that's what I needed to do.

I prayed, "Jesus, I have tried to be a good wife and mother. But I have done it my way. I didn't know how to do it before with your help but now I know. So I surrender my life, my marriage, and my children to you and ask you to teach me how to be a good wife and mother in a way that pleases you. I give you control of my life. Please teach me how to live your way. I surrender to you knowing full well that I have not done a good job of it in the past on my own."

As I finished my prayer, I heard over and over within my spirit, "It is done. It is done." After a while I realized the Holy Spirit was speaking about my eternity. It was secure because my name had been written in the Lamb's Book of Life, as the Bible indicates (Revelation 21:27 - RSV). Scripture also tells us that there is great rejoicing in heaven among the saints and angels when one repentant sinner comes to Jesus (Luke 15:7 – RSV). I had come to know and accept him as Savior and now I would grow and learn of Jesus as my Lord also.

I learned the Holy Spirit is all that scripture tells us He is. He is Teacher, Helper, Counselor, Guide, and Lover. He reveals Jesus and the Father to us. In the early days I was eager to walk deeper in the Spirit. I acquired such a hunger for reading and learning more about the mysteries of God and his Word. I read everything I could get my hands on and God always supplied just the right book. Miraculously, what I read seemed to speak to my greatest need at the moment.

When I would go to a prayer meeting, someone would share a scripture or an experience with the Lord, or give a teaching that would speak directly to a problem or situation that I was dealing with. It would minister to me in just the way I needed.

I learned that the Holy Spirit also was the One who convicts us when we sin. And it wasn't long until I realized that when it came to revealing a sin in my life, I would choose the Holy Spirit's conviction first over any human being's judgment. When the Holy Spirit convicts us of sin, it is done in such a gentle non-accusing way. He throws light into dark areas of our soul so that we can see it for ourselves and turn to Him, confessing in sorrow, asking for His counsel and help. He is faithful to give us the truth about our sinfulness and how to overcome future temptations. He woos us to see our error and His love melts us. Actually, the Spirit's light floods our hearts and reveals the sin there. Human beings are not always so kind and loving in their approach to another's mistakes, often accusing and condemning. But the Holy Spirit will not condemn us when we are in the act of confessing sorrow for our mistakes. He is quick and faithful to forgive all our transgressions.

Since this initial spiritual experience, my heart's desire is to share the good news with every member of my family including the extended family. Some have received it and found this great treasure for themselves. Others, I fear, have remained skeptical, certain I am out of my mind and perhaps hoping that after a while I will come down to earth and quit disturbing them with this new spirituality. I am much grieved about the latter. I have cried often to God asking Him to help those I love to know Him and His awesome love and mercy for themselves. It has been much easier to pray for others since I learned that this is also the Lord's will for them. God delights to reveal Himself to each one of us and to fill us with His Holy Spirit. All we have to do is ask.

JERRY, IT IS NOT ABOUT YOU!

Jerry Porter

"As a child growing up," Jerry Porter relates, "I attended church regularly with my mother. But in all those hours spent in church I never was taught that Jesus loved me and cared enough to die for me."

After high school, church was no longer a part of Jerry's life. He made many mistakes while trying to find his way; it was a difficult period. He sought meaning in life from success in his business and his accomplishments. Jerry comments, "I thought it was all about me. I had no peace in my heart."

Jerry knows that God placed Julie, his wife, in his life at a time when he needed direction. He saw that Julie and her family had a faith that was real. From their example, Jerry began to understand that God wanted a personal relationship with him.

The couple began to attend a church that was vastly different from the one of Jerry's childhood. For the first time his pastor was someone to whom he could relate. Music had always been a big part of Jerry's life, and the music in his new church ministered to him. For the first time, Jerry began to understand that God wanted to be Lord in his life, but his old habits and insecurities made it difficult for

24

him to release control. He continued to believe that his success was secured by his own efforts. He was aware that he was living a selfish life but he could not seem to change. For the next twenty years Jerry struggled in his relationship with God.

Then, his business began to fail. He could not admit to himself or his family that he was going broke. He had spent the best years of his life working to establish himself in the music industry. Now everywhere he turned he found closed doors. Who could he turn to for advice? Where could he find the financial help he so desperately needed? He felt abandoned and alone.

In July of 1990 he checked into a hotel, planning to attend the National Music Trade Fair, wondering why he was even there. He had an appointment with a credit representative from his major supplier. What would he tell him? He had no answers anymore. He put off the interview until the last day of the Fair. All too soon that moment arrived.

As Jerry dressed for the appointment, he was a physical and emotional wreck. His stomach was in knots and his loneliness weighed upon him like an invisible cloak. He pictured his family at home, going through their routines, totally unaware of how desperate the situation was. Then, for some reason, in the final moments before he left, Jerry lay down on the bed and closed his eyes. "Lord, please make something good come from this day," he prayed in sincerity.

The response was immediate. A feeling of calm settled over Jerry, and his heart was at peace. *Suddenly he was drenched*. His head was wet; his shirt was soaked. He felt cleansed, from the inside out. A smile lit his face and he suddenly felt confident and without a worry in the world. He thought to himself, "This is *total peace*." Quickly he changed his clothes and headed to the talk with his supplier.

As he strode along he spotted the *Kawai America* show room. On impulse he went in, thinking that he would say hello to their representative, someone he had known for years. When he asked for his friend, he was astounded to learn he had retired. "You've got to be kidding," Jerry mused aloud.

"Why? Do you still want to get on the road and into wholesale?" one of Jerry's other friends, who also worked for Kawai, asked. "I believe they just hired a guy, but…" At that moment the vice president of the company walked through the door, and Jerry's acquaintance turned and pointed toward Jerry, "Hey, this is the guy you should have hired."

The executive looked Jerry over, and talked to him briefly. A short time later Jerry left the showroom amazed that a miracle had happened. He not only knew he was going to be hired by this premier music company, but he realized that God had heard his desperate prayer. The Lord's timing was perfect and He was giving Jerry a fresh start.

Jerry has been with *Kawai America* for twenty-two years, and he has prospered. He often thinks about the dramatic answer to prayer he had that day in his lonely hotel room, and it humbles him.

He reflects, "I have often wished I could recapture that experience. Maybe it was a once in a lifetime thing, I'm not sure." What Jerry does know is that he may temporarily try to do things on his own and usually that is when he says he messes up. He explains, "I just know God is always there, tapping me on the shoulder saying, 'Jerry… it is not about you.'"

THE FAITHFULNESS OF JESUS

Ortha Parmelee

"I don't know what it's like *not* to be a Christian. I mean, I was always in a Christian environment," Ortha Parmelee told women at a church retreat. She remembered a childhood of family worship, regular church and Sunday school attendance, and the excitement of Methodist camp meetings.

At about age eleven Ortha went forward to the altar to publicly confess Jesus Christ as her Savior at an evangelistic meeting. "It was an emotional decision, I'm sure, and I can't recall that it made a great change in my life at the time," Ortha commented honestly. However, the lasting effects of that decision, and the faithfulness of Christ throughout her life was something Ortha wanted family and friends to know.

In her junior year of high school, Ortha realized, in a very personal way, that God had a purpose for her life. She was gravely ill with pneumonia at that time, and the country doctor, who had come to the farmhouse to care for her, was unable to bring her temperature down. In desperation he decided to consult another doctor, but Ortha's mother, Anna, asked him to wait a couple of hours. She had another idea.

Anna summoned three friends from her prayer group and the women laid hands on Ortha and prayed. In another room, her parents and two brothers knelt by the bed and earnestly interceded.

When the doctor returned—without saying a word to anyone—he rushed up the stairs to take his patient's pulse and temperature. By that time Ortha had returned to consciousness, recognizing her family and the doctor standing around the bed. As every-one looked on in awe at the young woman's returning awareness of her surroundings, Anna related to the physician how the women had come and they had all prayed for Ortha.

"Give anyone the glory, but she's better!" the gruff doctor retorted.

"Even though I was not totally aware of all that happened," Ortha remembered, "I realized in that moment that the Lord had spared my life and He must have a plan for me. I had accepted Him as my Savior and He was faithfully taking care of me."

Ortha married LeRoy Parmelee, a local sports hero, in 1942 when he was at the height of his baseball career as a pitcher with the New York Giants. Their lives revolved around major league games that were played seven days a week during the season. Because of the schedule and frequent moves, it was hard to sink down roots, and they stopped attending church. When their first child was born, Ortha and LeRoy bought a house in their hometown of Lambertville, Michigan and were able to spend six months of the year there. "Again, the Lord was faithful in His love and guidance—blessing us with a child to lead us back to Him," Ortha recalled. The new mother resolved to educate her son in the Christian faith and began faithfully to take him to Sunday school and church.

Two more children were born. By now it was 1943, the world was at war, and Le Roy left baseball to work in a factory that made war materials.

Social life for the Parmelees included partying with friends in homes and local taverns where "social drinking" was routine. While some of their friends drank too much, Ortha did not suspect at the time that her husband had a problem with alcohol. In telling about those years, Ortha said, "I was living a dual existence—one related to the activities of the Christian church, which had always been a part of my life…—and the other worldly one, and all that that implies. I'm sure that many times I stood up in church and sang, *What a friend we have in Jesus,* and then many days passed when I didn't even talk to Him, my best friend!" When LeRoy was offered a career promotion that required a move to another town, Ortha welcomed the change.

In their new home, the Parmelees joined a church and became active in the community. LeRoy continued to enjoy "a few beers" after work and on weekends. At first, Ortha would join him in local bars, bringing the children. "I remember feeling sorry for married men, sitting at the bar alone and rather forlorn looking, but again the Lord made a change in my life—He led me back to teaching. I felt a teacher should be a good example, so I no longer went with my husband to the taverns."

While he honored her convictions, LeRoy did not see why this should affect him. He enjoyed time spent in bars while increasingly Ortha chose a life which revolved around the church, her teaching career, and the children's activities.

About this time there occurred a great change in Ortha's life. She was attending a meeting with ladies from her church when she was called to the phone and LeRoy broke the news—her father had died. Ortha was in shock! Even though her father was elderly and frail, he had not been ill. The next day, after spending the night with her mother and making arrangements for the funeral, she returned home for a change of clothes. Alone at last, she gave into her grief. She loved her father dearly and respected him so much. She missed him already. She wept the cry of the broken-hearted.

"Suddenly I felt a Presence—it was as if someone had put His arm around my shoulders," Ortha remembered. "I felt calm and a peace such as I had never known… and from that moment my life was changed." Ortha returned to her family for the funeral, able to pray out loud, something she had never done before. Her mother and her aunt commented it was evident she was different.

"*He touched me,*" Ortha testified. "Again the Lord was faithful in keeping His promise to send a comforter. Gradually I came to understand what it meant to be a new person in Christ. Growth was gradual," she reiterated, "and I continue to learn how much He loves me."

The guidance of the Holy Spirit now helped her to cope with many distressing situations, not the least of which was her hurt and shame from LeRoy's increasing dependence on alcohol. While he loved his family dearly, his life revolved around his drinking. His son, Roy, was an outstanding high school basketball player. LeRoy admitted to Ortha that a neighbor had commented, "I don't understand you. I attend all the games and I don't even have a son playing, and yet you never come to watch your son play." As the addiction grew worse, Ortha shared her anguish with her daughter, Jan, on a visit to Colombia, where Jan was serving in the Peace Corps. Ortha told her daughter how her father, coming home from an afternoon of drinking, often fell by the back door. On days when Ortha was still at work a neighborhood couple would get him up and bring him in the house.

Later, after he retired, Ortha kept his whiskey in the basement where problems with his hip and knees precluded him from being able to get it. Ortha would try to parcel it out so as to keep him sober. At one point, when he had pestered and pestered her for a drink, in exasperation, Ortha said, "Choose me or the alcohol." He told her his choice was made; he would choose alcohol.

Different family members also tried to get him to acknowledge the problem, but such sessions ended in frustration and tears. Ortha commented, "The saddest experience is to see one you love wasting his life and talents. The Bible says we become a slave to that which controls us."

During these difficult years Ortha turned to God for direction and strength. "Had it not been for the guidance of the Holy Spirit in my life during this time, I could have been devastated, but He gave me the power and insight to become my own person. I drew comfort from the scriptures. Remember the parable of the lost sheep in Matthew 18:12-14? I knew it was not my Lord's will that my husband perish."

In 1971 the children suggested a plan of prayer intervention for their father. Ortha joined them in an agreement to pray for LeRoy at noon each day during their lunch hours. Their prayers continued daily for almost a year. The next summer their daughter, Jan, visited her parents for several weeks, convinced that God was ready to move. On a summer afternoon LeRoy's children and Ortha joined him in his favorite spot in the kitchen where he agreed to let them pray for him, saying, "I've never turned down anyone who wanted to pray for me."

Jan described the atmosphere of that time in prayer: "The love of God was like a blanket which covered us as we prayed. I have to believe that all of us, including Dad, felt it. I spoke out boldly in prayer, 'I take authority, in the name of the Lord Jesus Christ and I command the spirit of alcohol addiction to leave my father.' Dad held my hands in a vise-like grip, but even though I prayed this several times I didn't sense that anything had changed."

Following Jan's return to Virginia, Ortha's daughter, Annalee, suggested to her mother that her dad's frequent falls at home could possibly be a diabetic reaction to alcohol, and that when he fell, he needed immediate medical attention. As Ortha was cleaning one morning shortly thereafter, the impression was especially strong that the next time he collapsed she was to call an ambulance so he could be taken to the hospital.

Meanwhile in Virginia, after fasting for several days, Jan felt the peace of answered prayer. She called her brother, Roy, and he counseled her that often an answer in the spiritual realm is not seen immediately in the physical realm. He encouraged her, "Continue to wait on God and rest."

Three months passed, and then one day LeRoy fell. Ortha had never been able to lift his dead weight before—he weighed well over 200 pounds. Miraculously, that day she was able to raise him up and put him to bed. As she walked away the Holy Spirit spoke to her, "I told you not to get him up and to call an ambulance!" Ortha went to the phone near the downstairs bedroom and told her husband, "I am calling an ambulance to take you to the hospital."

"I won't go!" he told her furiously. In the past she would have yielded, but on this day she had the courage to make the call. When the ambulance crew arrived, LeRoy refused to get on the stretcher. Ortha said to him, "Doc (her favorite name for him), if you love me—you will get on the stretcher." Wordlessly he lay down.

LeRoy had been doctoring with a physician who prescribed medicine over the phone. Previously, the family had secretly met with the doctor to ask that he see his patient. They wanted him to be aware he was treating an alcoholic. The doctor had been sympathetic but continued as before. The day LeRoy was admitted to the hospital, his doctor's father had a heart attack and the physician was already on a plane to California to be with his father. In the absence of his primary care physician, the chief surgeon at the hospital took over LeRoy's care.

Ortha told the surgeon that LeRoy must have alcohol. The doctor assured her that while they would give his patient every help to dry him out—vitamin B shots, for example—they would not give him alcohol. When LeRoy was released from the hospital two weeks later, no medication had been necessary. All desire for alcohol had simply left him.

The new doctor adjusted LeRoy's previous prescriptions, some of which had certainly contributed to his feelings of depression. LeRoy returned home with a new lease on life. In conversations with his family he affirmed the decision made as a child to accept Jesus Christ as his Savior. He lived eight years in sobriety before his death. During those years he enjoyed life and his family.

One of his pleasures was to call in to radio broadcasts and exchange stories, with his marvelous wit, about his baseball career. His desire for alcohol had so disappeared that he boasted he was able to keep beer in the refrigerator to offer a neighbor next door who liked to have one after he had mowed the lawn.

One day he mentioned to his family he had received a request for an autograph from a Christian man who was dying of cancer. "I wrote and told him," Le Roy said, "if you are a Christian, then you do not need to be afraid of death." This response comforted the family. They understood that LeRoy was at peace about his own future following death. He died at age seventy four.

Ortha outlived LeRoy by twenty five years. When she died two months before her hundredth birthday, many people from the church and community joined her family to mourn her passing. In her Bible, well-worn and underlined, was taped this scripture: "But this I call to mind, and therefore I have hope: the steadfast love of the Lord never ceases, His mercies never come to an end; they are new every morning; great is thy faithfulness." (Lamentations 3:21 – 23 RSV)

THE GENTLE CALL OF GOD

Rev. Robert Malsack

The golfers, an odd assortment of teen-agers and adults, joked and laughed together as they formed in groups to tee off. They gathered to celebrate the retirement of Reverend Bob Malsack with a charity golf tournament. An unusual sight awaited them on the greens: signs imprinted with Bible verses, stuck into the ground on two wire legs. *"Beloved, let us love one another, because love is from God."* (1 John 4:7 NRSV) *"God's love was revealed among us in this way: God sent his only Son into the world so that we might live through him."* (1 John 4:9) *"There is no fear in love, because love casts out all fear."* (1 John 4:18). Here was yet just another expression of the clergyman's faith, typically making God's love real to people in the community.

"Pastor Bob," as he is widely known, was a mentor to young men at the local high school, where he served as assistant football coach. He worked diligently in the weight room, sweating along with the young athletes. When they had a problem, he was available to offer a listening ear or a quiet word of encouragement. When the high school determined they could no longer observe baccalaureate because of its religious emphasis, some students came to Pastor Bob, expressing their outrage. Rather than make it a political issue, he reminded them that no one could keep them from praying if that's what they wanted to do. And, by the way, if they were seeking a place to have baccalaureate, his church would welcome them and their parents. The idea resonated with the seniors and the practice continues each spring in area churches.

Vacation Bible School was one of his favorite summer activities. The staff included him in skits as different characters, to the delight of the children. One year he willingly portrayed a naturally bald-headed "Mr. Clean".

He and Father Jim from St. Rita Catholic Church were like brothers, reaching out to their fellow clergymen in the community for a monthly luncheon and combined celebrations of Lent and Easter. When Father Jim became fatally ill with cancer, he exhorted Pastor Bob, who was considering moving, to stay in Brooklyn. Bob must continue to lead the ecumenical community they had begun together, Father Jim insisted. Pastor Bob promised his friend he would do this—and he continued to minister in Brooklyn for over twenty-seven years, long after Father Jim's death.

The stories people tell, both within his congregation and in the wider community, are endless: moments when tragedy struck, Pastor Bob was there; throughout family crises, he lent support; and the compassion of that other caring Shepherd shone through in Bob's willingness to lay down his life—and his time—for the sheep. Now the unbelievable was happening: Pastor Bob was leaving to serve as an interim pastor in Texas and eventually retire from the ministry.

As a young boy, Robert Malsack never considered becoming a minister. He enjoyed listening to the broadcasts of the Assembly of God preacher from down the street and nationally known evangelist, Oral Roberts. He was a faithful member of the church where his mother played the organ—but as a teenager he chose not to attend youth group because the "cool kids" didn't go. Besides, he never knew a preacher that he identified with in a *personal* way.

The first prompting to consider the ministry came on Youth Sunday at Bob's home church. A worship service traditionally led by college students, none of the students wanted to preach the sermon. Perhaps remembering the style of the preachers he admired, Bob, now a student at the university, volunteered to speak. The congregation listened in amazement at his gifted preaching. Afterward, the pastor approached Bob to ask if he had ever considered becoming a minister. Bob answered politely that he had other plans, but he thought silently, "No way!" For one thing, his decision to follow a pre-medicine discipline had greatly pleased his father.

In college Bob labored faithfully in his science and anatomy courses, achieving excellent grades. Meanwhile, he decided to take a course in the "Bible as Literature." He felt drawn to the professor, but more importantly, Bob was fascinated as Bible passages came alive. It was also during this time that the idea of going into the ministry began to tug on his consciousness. When he failed repeatedly to pass the medical college admissions exam, his Bible professor suggested there might be a reason for this obstacle blocking his path. Did God have some other plan for him? Bob wondered.

It was at this time Bob's pastor gave an unprecedented altar call. Although he did not go forward, Bob committed his life to the Lord. He reports, "I told God, 'if you want me to be a doctor, then you make me a doctor – and if not, make me what <u>You</u> want me to be.'"

There was one major hurdle. Some years before Bob's father and mother had divorced, and while Bob lived with his mother, his dad's approval was important to him. When Bob told his father that he wanted to become a doctor, he could tell his dad was proud. Shortly after his prayer for God's direction, Bob was sitting in his dad's den when his father asked him, "Bob, I gotta know if you want to get into medical school because I need to get the money. I *know* I can get you in." Bob knew his father was someone who believed that whatever you wanted you could buy, if you had enough cash. Then suddenly in an affectionate tone his dad added, "What I want you to be—is happy."

At that moment Bob made his decision. "I want to be a minister."

His father was a bit flustered, "I don't know that I can help you there," he said. But his father did help him, Bob would tell— he paid Bob's way through seminary.

When the time came for Bob to look for a church in which to serve, not feeling overly confident, he began applying for associate pastor positions but without success. Once again, God supplied just the right nudge to move him forward. His mother and step-father had come to California to visit. When Bob told them he was looking for associate pastor appointments, his step-father, a construction worker, told him bluntly, "Ah boloney! Take a small church and learn how to do it while you go." Miraculously and unsolicited, soon thereafter, a small church in Lindsay, California, extended a call to the seminary graduate, and taking his step-father's advice, he accepted the position.

He served the little church for three years. "The congregation was very kind to me," he said. "They understood my differences, my youthfulness, and they 'grew me up.' Because they were patient with me, I did not become sour in the ministry like so many of the young pastors I met."

After three years in Lindsey, Bob and his wife, Marsha, with their two young children wanted to relocate near grandparents in Michigan. Bob contacted an old friend, the senior pastor of the church in Pasadena which he had attended as a seminarian. The gentleman was now the Executive Presbyter of the Lake Michigan Presbytery, responsible for the administration of sixty-six Presbyterian churches. That Christmas he set up three appointments for Bob while he and Marsha were visiting family in Michigan. All three interviews, as Bob describes them, were disasters. At the first, by his own admission,

Bob's sermon was boring. At the second, people did not even stay to interview him, and at the third, while they took him out to lunch, one by one the committee excused themselves and left Bob sitting there.

As they packed to return to California, he and Marsha agreed to return in the summer because her father's health was fragile, but discouraged by Bob's rejections, they determined not to seek further interviews in Michigan.

When summer came, Bob did not alert his mentor at the Presbytery that he was coming to Michigan. However, upon arrival he did call him, out of friendship, telling him he was in town and would be glad to schedule lunch at his convenience. Then he and Marsha went out to eat.

When they returned, there was a message on the answering machine saying, "You have an interview with the Presbyterian Church in Brooklyn on Thursday and you are scheduled to preach on Sunday." Bob looked at Marsha and said, "Out of respect, we have to make an appearance."

On Thursday night they met the committee from Brooklyn at the home of the chairman. The committee had had no warning either. They had interviewed various candidates for two years with no success, and this young man from California came like a bolt out of the blue. Not only were they not interested in considering someone from that far away, but they had no information on him except that the Executive Presbyter had scheduled this encounter.

Bob, who always prefers people who are "real," was delighted when one of the committee members, a teacher of aerobic exercise, was encouraged by those present to give a demonstration. From there everyone got to know each other, and visited until long after dark.

Bob preached on Sunday and afterwards, the committee extended the call for him to be their pastor, all in a matter of four days. Concerned that he not be misled by the suddenness of events, Bob called an elderly pastor colleague when he returned to California.

"Can I know this is God's call?" the young man asked his senior mentor.

The experienced man chuckled as he answered, "Only because it happened that fast can you be sure it was God's will. If it was human effort, it would go on for weeks!"

Now as he looked back over his twenty seven years of ministry in the church at Brooklyn, Pastor Bob was asked, "How did you know God was calling you into the ministry and how did you come to Brooklyn?" Bob answers, "It came gently, one small decision at a time." And isn't that how God leads us all—gently, one decision at a time.

HEALED AND RESTORED

Carol's Story

"I can't believe you are so *stupid*, Carol!* *What* do you have for brains? You are *always* thinking about *yourself*." Tom's* words raged, his every syllable, propelled like an arrow from his powerful, practiced bow of abuse, piercing his wife's vulnerable heart with scorn and contempt.

Carol came from a sheltered home, surrounded by love. When she was thirteen, her father died and the loss of the person she idolized, shattered Carol's secure world. She closed her heart, refusing to grieve, angry at God and angry at her father for deserting her. This led to a time of hurt and insecurity.

She was just fifteen when she started dating Tom. He was a gifted, articulate senior in high school. He enjoyed her company and she was flattered by his attention. The warning signs were evident even then. Tom was addicted to pornography and living in a household where his father spoke harshly to his mother. But Carol ignored Tom's impatience and wounding remarks, telling herself he loved her and in time she would be able to change him.

* Not the real names.

At eighteen Carol married Tom, but from the beginning the marriage was a nightmare. Not only did her husband convince her that she caused every problem, but his obsession with pornography made intimacy difficult. In addition, his spending sprees left her feeling powerless to change her circumstances. When he struck her on two occasions, she threatened divorce. He never hit her again but the hurtful barrage of words continued, even in public. She tried to convince herself that he didn't mean what he said, but the situation grew worse.

The couple began to drink heavily, and increasingly Carol mirrored Tom's verbal abuse, using words to defend herself, calling him names. Desperate for help, she went to counseling and was told she should leave her husband. By now the couple had two children and Carol lacked confidence that she could support herself and the children.

Carol's family had taken her to church as a child. Now, she hungered for that sense of security and the loving presence of God. She found a church and began to attend regularly with her children. Sunday worship did not seem enough—she hungered for more of God. She joined a Bible study where the women prayed for one another.

During one prayer meeting one of the women described laying hands on her children when they were sick and watching as God healed. "Just pray for the Holy Spirit to fill you," she was told. "It's God's Spirit flowing through you that heals."

When her five year old daughter had a bad fall the next day, Carol's first thought was to call the doctor. But remembering the conversation in the prayer group, she laid her hands on the child's swollen and scratched face and prayed for God to heal her —and to fill Carol with His Holy Spirit. Carol felt a surge of power flow through her body, and her hands became so heated that her little girl exclaimed, "Mommy, your hands are so hot!" Suddenly, Carol *knew* that Jesus Christ was *alive*. In a short time, all swelling gone and the bruises beginning to fade, Carol's daughter went out to play. This was a life-changing experience for Carol.

Carol began to beseech God to help with her home situation. She prayed, "Lord, put a guard on my mouth." She sought daily to forgive Tom for his behavior and to look at his many positive points. Daily she asked God's forgiveness for her own angry reactions and the desire to retaliate. Carol found support in the Christian community and began to clearly hear God's voice guiding and caring for her.

For the first time, she began to grieve her father's death. As she allowed herself to mourn, God's comfort softened her heart and He began to show her how precious she was to Him.

Tom's job required that he travel, and Carol looked forward to these absences. However, when he returned the hellish existence continued; not only was Tom abusive toward her but also toward their children.

While Tom's hurtful attacks on his family did not seem to change, he became active in their neighborhood church. Carol continued to go with him, but her experiences with healing and the other gifts of the Spirit, led her to find additional support in a Pentecostal church. One night as she knelt at the altar, the pain of the years of abuse seemed to rise in an inescapable wave of emotion. Once she began to weep it seemed that there was no stopping the sobs that rose from the depth of her being. Afterwards, she felt cleansed and the prayers of those ministering to her at the altar brought healing and fresh strength to her soul.

Then one day, after the children were grown, it was as if a dam burst. With the latest evidence of a spending spree leaving them thousands of dollars in debt, Carol cried out to God in desperation, "*Get him out of my life, God! I don't want him.*" She decided to file for divorce. When she signed the papers, she felt as if a huge weight were lifted off her shoulders. Tom was totally shocked when he learned of the pending divorce. He begged her to stay, went before the church and confessed his emotional abuse. He asked her before witnesses to reconsider. Moved by his fear and promises to seek God's help to change, Carol dropped the divorce proceedings. The two of them attended counseling, and on a DeColores spiritual retreat weekend, Tom asked Jesus into his heart. Carol's faith was encouraged as she watched God working in her husband's life. For the next year their home situation improved.

However, in spite of his desire to change, Tom began to be pulled back into pornography and he returned increasingly to his abusive behavior toward Carol. Desperate once more, convicted by the fury of her own reactions, Carol prayed, *"Change me, God!"* God gave her a vision of a storm. The waves of the storm threatened to overwhelm Carol and her husband but miraculously they remained safe. A couple of months later, doctors diagnosed Tom with an aggressive cancer.

During the next two years of caring for him, Carol saw many positive changes in Tom as he prepared himself for death. Then one spring day while he was running an errand, Tom collapsed and died suddenly from a blood clot in his leg.

That following summer, Carol, troubled by pain in her wrist, prayed for healing and heard the Holy Spirit tell her, "You are resentful."

Surprised, Carol asked, "About what?"

"You are resentful against Tom for all the hurt he caused you in the marriage."

Recognizing the truth, Carol boldly prayed, "Lord, take this resentment from me; I do not want it." Thinking this would take care of the problem, she was dismayed when the pain not only became worse but spread to her shoulders, arms and legs. After suffering for several days, she asked in desperation, "Lord, what is going on?"

"Ask for forgiveness," was the thought brought to her mind.

Now, in humility she prayed, "Lord, forgive me for I have sinned in holding onto resentment against Tom." Expecting now to feel clean, she was puzzled that she still struggled. Finally, she realized that she had to give memories of past injuries and negative thoughts about her husband and her marriage *daily* to the Lord. Although she had believed that Tom's death brought an end to all of her suffering, God was showing her that she had more work to do. She needed to allow the Holy Spirit to work at a deeper level, to help her forgive Tom, to let go of the past, and to receive additional healing.

Carol made a conscious decision to let go of resentment and bitterness. "I give this to you, Jesus," was the prayer Carol prayed for eight months whenever negative thoughts intruded.

Gradually, Carol began to thank God that through her marriage to Tom, she received two beautiful children and three granddaughters. She could thank God for her marriage to Tom and what it taught her. Because Carol was obedient to forgive and let go of resentment from the past, God was able to heal her damaged emotions. Today she is re-married to a Christian man who honors God in his life and marriage, and Carol is enjoying all the blessings of a second chance at happiness. *To God be the glory.*

EVALYNE ONSTED

THE QUILT LADY

The two little girls stood in a room where every inch of space held a doll—each one more lovely than the next. Evalyne was awed at the sight; she had never seen such treasures! With wonder she reached out and picked up one of the dolls. Her cousin, an only child, gave her a look that said, "How dare you touch something that belongs only to me!" Later, the women became close friends, but on this day Evalyne's heart was broken.

"My cousin never said a word but the expression on her face and the way she looked at me said it all," Evalyne related. "I didn't say anything to her either—I just got up and left. As I walked back to my grandparents, I began to cry. When I told my grandmother what happened, she said, 'You stay here with me, Honey.'"

From her back room Evalyne's grandmother took some fabric blocks and showed her granddaughter how to embroider pieces for a quilt. Evalyne worked on the quilt through the years and finally finished it shortly after she married.

That painful encounter and her grandmother's understanding response led to a lifelong love of quilting for Evalyne Onsted. Thousands of fabrics came together in exquisite patterns and textures under her artistic eye and expert needle. The hand-stitched quilts were presented as gifts to charities, soldiers, and anyone needing comfort. And quilts have ministered to Evalyne in her darkest hours.

During Evalyne's eighteenth summer, she worked for a family in Michigan at Loon Lake where she met "that handsome fellow," Ross, who became her husband. Their first son, Darrel, was born in January of 1943. The nation was at war and although his son was still an infant, Ross had his heart set on enlisting in the Air Corps. When he asked her what she thought, Evalyne supported his decision to enlist. When he returned, their second son, Gary, was born.

Son Gary became an advocate for her richly colored and textured needlework. It was he who built her quilting frame and the table for cutting out squares. In his twenties he went off to war, like his father before him, but in his case, the conflict was in Viet Nam and when he returned he was never the same. He married and had two children, but his health was fragile.

His mother finally saw into his wounded soul after his father's death in June of 2001. One day as she sat at the kitchen table, he joined her, put his head down and wept, saying, "After Nam, I thought I was immune to death, but when it hits you so close, it's just hard to bear." He sobbed and sobbed as if his heart would break.

He went on to tell her that in Viet Nam he had two buddies. One left home while his wife was expecting their first child. Each day this comrade wanted to know the date so he could figure how close they were to his baby's arrival. His other buddy was a stand-out football player, four years of college and two years in the pros. He looked forward to returning to the States to play football.

Then one day, as the three soldiers were on patrol, bullets started to fly in every direction. Gary hit the dirt, and as he lay there, he realized his friends would not ever see their dreams realized: one would never know he was a father, and the other would never play football again. As he lay there, he cried, "Lord, why not me? Why… not… *me?*"

"After he told me that, I thought about it for a few days," Evalyne said. "Then, I went to him and told him, 'God knew I needed you. That's why your life was spared.'"

Over the last few months of 2006 Evalyne had a nine square pattern on the quilting frame and Gary would often say, "It's almost done, isn't Mom?" He seemed to take special interest in the beautiful colors as they came together. Over a six month period he had severe back pain, and when he went to the doctor, they told him the bad news. He had lung cancer, cancer of the liver, and cancer in his bones. Because he had been in Viet Nam, they suspected it was due to exposure to Agent Orange.

As Gary lay in the hospital under hospice care, Evalyne went to see him. She was amazed at the thoughtful beauty of the room. It was furnished comfortably with a couch that could be made into a bed, upholstered chairs, lamps on the tables—then she looked again because at the foot of his bed, a quilt lay folded. At first she wasn't quite sure because the coverlet had been washed so many times, but when she picked it up, she saw her first impression had been correct. The quilt was the same pattern as the one at home on the frame her son had built. As she looked at it, she thought, "That's love sent by somebody."

"Gary died so fast," his mother recalled.

The day after Gary died, Evalyne's Pastor called to ask how he was. "I've been gone a week, and I just wondered how Gary is doing?" he said.

Evalyne's voice was soft as she recounted her reply to the pastor. "He died. He is in a better place, and he won't suffer anymore."

"And that is what I believe," she would state emphatically.

The quilt on the frame is done now. Evalyne says she will never give it away because every time she looks at it she thinks of Gary, so proud of her quilting, saying, "It's almost done now, Mom. It's almost done."

There is one other quilt Evalyne has not given away, and that is the first one she made with the quilt squares her grandmother gave her. The figures of children in turn-of-the-century clothing are embroidered with the same original stitches but when she began to quilt in earnest, she took the old coverlet apart and put it together again, "As it should have been done." However, the embroidery stitches are still those done by the little girl whose hurting heart was given new direction by her grandmother's loving instruction and God's guiding hand.

Evalyne's first quilt with an embroidered quilt top

The quilt Evalyne's son Gary so admired.

SHELTERED BY PRAYER

Mary Ann and Theresa Allore's story

"You are lying! I don't believe the baby is even mine."

Theresa closed her eyes, the pain of rejection and betrayal cutting her to the heart. The agony was excruciating. She couldn't breathe. How could this be happening? How could she have been so naïve? The weight of what lay ahead threatened to crush her, and the man she thought would be committed to her "till death do us part," had abandoned her just when she needed him most.

The summer before, Theresa had a landed a job in the university hospital lab. It had been a wonderful opportunity for her to use the training she received in her courses and it would help her get a good job when she graduated. It was during that summer that she met Mike, who was taking classes on campus. She was attracted to this musician who wrote beautiful songs about his Christian faith. Before the summer was over they talked of marriage and traveled to meet each other's families. When the fall semester drew near, Mike received the discouraging news that he had failed all his classes. He decided to return home to California to attend a university there, planning to return the following semester. He called Theresa daily and they looked forward to his being on campus again so they could be together.

About two weeks after his departure, Theresa began to be nauseous and suspected she was pregnant. A week later the laboratory test confirmed her suspicions. When she called Mike, although initially sympathetic, his response to the presence of a child was not what she expected. He was adamant that he did not want his family to know.

"I could marry you but it probably wouldn't last more than five years," he told her coldly. Theresa remembered meeting his sister who was single with two children, and the truth of his plans began to appear vastly different from his promises.

"I will find someone to help you take care of it," he offered in another conversation. In shock Theresa realized he was talking about an abortion. She had always thought Mike was against abortion.

In the silence that followed his advice Mike added, "I have had to take care of things like this before."

Theresa was stunned! Where was the thoughtful, caring young man she had spent time with these last several months? How could she have trusted him? His true character was now revealed and she was devastated.

Though she believed in her heart that abortion was wrong, the temptation to escape the repercussions of her actions threatened to overwhelm her. The words "take care of it" started to stick in her head. Mike was obviously not going to give her any support if she decided to keep the baby. How would she cope, attending classes, pregnant and alone these next nine months? She was a junior. Would the responsibilities of caring for her child keep her from finishing her degree? Would she have to give up her dreams of a career and move home?

Knowing how supportive her own parents were in a crisis, she could not believe that Mike's parents should be ignorant of the couple's dilemma. However, when she called his mother, Mike was furious—and so their last conversation ended with his accusation that she was lying and the baby was not his child. Theresa was never to hear from Mike again.

Meanwhile, Theresa's parents, Bernie and Mary Ann, were thankful that everything was peaceful in the family. Their four daughters were busy with school activities and their oldest, Theresa, was away studying at the university. When someone in their parish prayer group asked for people willing to commit to three days of fasting and prayer for women considering an abortion, they were willing. Besides, they were definitely against abortion. They began to fast and pray.

Back at the dorm Theresa prayed in desperation, "Look God, I know what you *want* me to do, but I don't think I have the strength to get through it." She thought of having to tell her parents about the pregnancy, afraid it would kill them. "God, be *very clear* and give me what I need to do the right thing," she pleaded.

That very morning at breakfast, as she sat across from her friend Joyce in the cafeteria, she noticed Joyce was wearing a small pin with two tiny feet. When she asked about it Joyce explained, "Oh, these feet are the same size as a two month old baby before it's born." Theresa was astounded! No one at school knew she was pregnant—nor that the baby growing in her womb was now two months old.

Still stubbornly struggling, every time she turned around that day Theresa ran into people handing out pro-life pamphlets and having pro-life discussions. Absorbed as she was in her own problems, it was not until later she realized that the Christian campus was in the middle of a big Pro-Life Weekend. By the end of the day Theresa was convinced that God had made His way abundantly clear to her. She was not alone and God would provide the strength and resources to both help her through the pregnancy and nurture and care for her child. It was time to tell her parents.

The third day of the fast had arrived and Bernie and Mary Ann got a phone call that their daughter was catching a ride with some friends and was coming home for the weekend. They had not seen her for many months because of her job during the summer. While they had been glad about her career opportunity, they missed her and were excited she was coming home for a visit.

They hurried around, prepared a nice meal, and tidied up the house for her arrival. Theresa and her friends finally arrived and they had a good visit, but something didn't seem right. Bernie and Mary Ann sensed something was wrong. Finally, their daughter took them aside and told them the unexpected news. She was pregnant, and the young man she had hoped to marry wanted nothing to do with the baby. He had suggested she have an abortion and offered to pay for it.

Theresa confessed that she had been tempted, but it was against everything she believed. When she refused to have the abortion, her boyfriend became angry and told her he would not admit to being the father of the child. Parents and daughter cried together, but at the same time, her parents were so thankful. Their prayers had been answered. When their daughter was tempted, she had the strength to say no to abortion. Unknowingly, they had been praying for their own daughter during the period of fasting and prayer.

God gave Bernie and Mary Ann the strength to forgive and support Theresa through the months ahead. She went back to the university, and persevered to the end of the school year. It was a difficult time for her, but four days after she finished her junior year she gave birth to a beautiful son.

She spent the summer at home with her parents, and then she returned to the university to finish her senior year.

Although her parents offered to take care of the baby, Theresa felt he was her responsibility. Besides, she loved him with all her heart and she could not imagine life without him. She rented an apartment with her younger sister who was just starting her university career as a freshman. Theresa worked and went to classes, putting her baby in day care part of the time, and receiving additional babysitting help from her sister. It was not an easy year but all went well: Theresa graduated with honors and was hired immediately by Johns Hopkins Hospital in Baltimore. And God was faithful—lovingly guiding her path. Four years later, she married a fine Christian man who loved her and her son.

Finally, Mary Ann summarizes: "Chris, our grandson, was a happy child and is a joy to all our family. He graduated from college in 2006 and is a very responsible person. Thank God, Theresa didn't decide that abortion would solve her problems, but put everything in God's hands. Bernie and I are very grateful that we took time to fast and pray for those with the greatest decision of their lives...to save a life."

SEEING THROUGH THE LENS OF FAITH

Gary M. Jones

In April 2006 my wife, Jean, and I, along with fifteen fellow Presbyterians embarked on a mission trip to aid with hurricane relief in Bay St. Louis, Mississippi. Some were from other churches in the area, strangers at the onset of our journey, while others who attended our church in Brooklyn, Michigan, were little more than acquaintances. However, by the time of our return nine days later we shared a bond created by God that can never be broken.

We caravanned in four vehicles and after two long days of driving we arrived at the First Presbyterian Church which had been converted to serve as one of many command centers in the area.

The sanctuary was the only part of the church that was still recognizable for its original purpose. The kitchen had become a mess hall set up to feed the large number of volunteers. A large mess tent occupied the area immediately outside the kitchen. A wooden walk led past the mess tent to the shower tents. Further back was "tent city," where side by side stood dozens of four and six man tents which served as sleeping quarters for those who preferred sleeping outside the church. Two toilets inside the church and four port-a-johns outside served the needs of as many as one hundred volunteers at various times.

Each morning after a brief worship service and breakfast, the daily assignments were given out. I was appointed to plumbing jobs along with Keith, a member of our Brooklyn group whom I had become acquainted with on our trip down. While plumbing was the one thing I put on my application that I would not want to do, I soon got over my reluctance and found that Keith and I worked well together. After a few days we became good friends, and I saw the assignment as a blessing.

As I went to work each day, I did not even consider that there might be problems with my eyesight. In 1995 I suffered a severe injury to my right eye which unfortunately was my good eye at the time. Surgery was required and a lens was implanted. Things did not go well and as a result my vision in that eye is blurry even when corrected with a contact lens. I am able to see well with contacts in both eyes, however, and now rely on my corrected left eye to do most of the work. I never considered there might be a problem in Mississippi.

On Wednesday morning after washing up in the bathroom and while attempting to put in my contacts, I lost my left lens, the one for my stronger eye. I was pretty sure I had dropped it in the sink because my finger and not the contact had touched my eye when I attempted to put it in. I began searching for it as best I could with no success. I asked my wife, Jean, for her help finding the missing lens. We retrieved a flashlight out of my tent and she checked my eye. My lenses are tinted blue so they are easy to see and I have on occasion had a lens slide to the side of my eye. Whenever this happened in the past, however, I have been able to feel the lens and with Jean's direction center it back on my eye. Unfortunately it was not there.

I recovered my spare lens case and held my breath. I had recently lost another lens and had not taken the time to replace it—and I was not sure which lens I had with me. As it turned out it was the right lens or in this instance, not the lens I needed. I was devastated. Since I had no other options, I inserted the spare right contact into my left eye. The results were not good. While better than no contact at all, my vision was blurry. I would be unable to read even large print material and certainly be of little or no help to perform the task we had been assigned.

At service that morning I prayed. "Lord, why has this happened now?" Not sensing an answer, I chose to surrender the situation to Him. "God, I am not sure how a blind man can be of use to You here, but I will do whatever You want me to do. I will accept whatever happens as Your will."

"I'll call my optometrist in Michigan as soon as they open," I promised Keith that morning, after recounting to him what had happened with my contact. "Perhaps they can ship replacements overnight to me here at the church."

Upon contacting my doctor's office later that day I was informed that because of my special prescription it would be a week before replacements would be available. I placed the order and said I would be in as soon as we got back to pick up the new lens. I continued to pray for an answer as to how I could function.

Later that morning, I was working in an unlit bathroom with Keith when I felt the contact shift off the center of my left eye. I had anticipated this and had brought my wetting solution, which I left in the car. I popped the lens out into my hand and asked Keith if he could see a contact there. I was so blind without the lens, I could not tell if there was a lens in my hand. He said that he could see a contact lens and so closing my hand lightly into a fist I went outside to retrieve my wetting solution and reinsert the lens. I opened the car door with my free hand and after securing the solution, slowly opened my right hand which contained the lens.

In the bright sunlight I immediately saw two lenses, both sitting face up side by side in my hand. I closed my hand and returned to the bathroom where Keith was still working and asked him again if he had seen a lens in my hand a minute earlier.

"Absolutely," he replied.

I then asked him how many lenses he had seen. While I was unable to clearly see his face in the darkened bathroom without my contacts, I was certainly able to discern the puzzlement in his voice as he assured me—there had been only one lens in my hand.

"Are you certain?" I asked.

"Absolutely," he replied yet again.

I asked him to step outside with me and I showed him the two lenses. We were both elated at God's marvelous answer to my prayer.

However, in the moment of seeing the extra contact lens I also understood the answer to a concern I had brought to God in the past.

I usually felt that God was listening and answering my concerns and questions as I prayed to Him. However, at other times He seemed distant and even perhaps *unavailable* or *busy*. "Perhaps," I would think, "this particular issue is something He considers unimportant and I should get past it and move on." Often, I would think how marvelous it must have been for those who were there to witness Jesus' miracles and to know He lived, because they had seen Jesus with their own eyes and heard Him with their own ears.

But at that moment, as I looked at those two wonderful, blue contact lenses in my hand, I understood something for the first time. Because we choose to love God and have faith in His grace and His love for us, we are precious to Him. It's the world and worldly things that distract us and interfere with our ability to sense Him with us at all times. It's like static on a radio or poor television reception due to the buildings around us and our distance from the transmitter. In this age of cable and satellite, I realize the latter concept may seem foreign to some. Nevertheless, what we need to do with our relationship with

God is eliminate the interference and get a cable connection with him as Lord of our lives. When we become more concerned for others than for ourselves; when we act with love; when we trust in God and remove the clutter of this world from our lives, we can see Him and will witness His miracles which are happening continuously, all around us. *I now saw.*

I inserted the lens and was able to continue with the repairs we had come to do. Even after returning to Michigan and picking up my new prescription, I continued to wear my "miracle" lens.

While I believe this was a miracle from God, it was only one of many we witnessed while in Bay St. Louis. The consideration and kindness we experienced and the smoothness with which the entire operation ran was nothing short of miraculous.

I now believe God is with us always and his supernatural interventions happen every day. All we have to do is eliminate the interference and create an environment where we can hear and witness His Grace and Love.

UNEXPECTED CONFIRMATIONS

Marilyn Troska

Drinking in cool breezes that stir the wisteria lattice overhead, and listening to chirping birds, Marilyn and her husband, Jim, sit on their deck, thankful for these calming sounds of nature. Without God's leading, they never would have left California to find this idyllic Michigan retirement home.

It seemed a disaster when Jim came home from work early in the fall of 1997, not to return again—downsized by the company where he had worked for seventeen years. Marilyn's thought that afternoon was, "This only happens to other families, not to ours!"

Although they weren't living paycheck to paycheck, their older daughter was in her final year of university and their younger daughter was a college freshman. They certainly weren't in a position to just sit back and think "retirement."

Even with the help of a professional job recruitment company, it took Jim six months to land a job that was eighty miles away. However, within a year, they cut his employment from five days a week to three and finally he was let go.

A job in Evansville, Indiana, sounded just right —until the first interview. Perhaps his full head of white hair made him look much older than his fifty seven years. "Age discrimination is alive and well in America!" Marilyn thought to herself when he wasn't hired. Then another position became a possibility: it seemed to fit his credentials perfectly and involved the shortest commute he had ever had. Nevertheless, during the first interview the recruiter admitted that a merger was forthcoming and they would actually not be hiring for some time.

Meanwhile, Jim, an avid outdoorsman, found the freeway traffic noise behind their Southern California home intolerable. He missed the stimulation of his colleagues at work, and the almost six foot brick wall in his backyard only increased his sense of isolation.

Adding to his discontent, his favorite hobby of fishing was limited to dropping his hook in the water one day a week at the Anaheim Water District's reservoir. He paid to fish the stocked pond along the expressway to the accompaniment of a constant roar of vehicles, a situation made more uncomfortable by the scorching California sun. Ocean fishing, while available, was not enjoyable either. The deep sea boat trips were expensive and loaded to capacity with people fishing elbow to elbow. This was nothing like the quiet trout streams of his past.

The thought of moving out of California to retire began to sound appealing. Certainly the cost of living might be cheaper elsewhere and a rural location would allow Jim to pursue his outdoor interests. The couple began to plan a trip to Michigan to check out the area called the Irish Hills. This region has a plethora of lakes within a ten mile radius, and the Great Lakes within driving distance. Jim reminded Marilyn that fishing season is much longer than most hunting seasons, and so the proximity of lakes was a particular blessing. However, hunting areas were also close so it seemed ideal for that hobby as well. More and more Michigan was looking like the logical choice for their retirement home.

Meanwhile, Marilyn was struggling with the thought of a move 2,100 miles away from their two daughters. At a Magnificat Prayer Breakfast one Saturday morning prayer teams extended the invitation for people to come forward for individual prayer. When Marilyn shared with the prayer team her concern, one of them asked her if she had relatives in Michigan. Marilyn replied, "Oh, yes, my brother and his family." When the woman asked if they were on good terms, Marilyn admitted truthfully, "No... *he hates my guts.*" After praying for her, the intercessor offered that she felt the Lord was going to use this move to heal the relationship between sister and brother. This reassured Marilyn. *Surely, the Lord was in the move.* Now, she was at peace.

Jim and Marilyn looked intensely for a lake home in August 2002, moving to the Irish Hills in May 2003. They took that winter to enjoy their last Christmas and Easter with their daughters, to go through twenty - five years of storage in their California home, and throw a farewell party, inviting family friends and neighbors.

The Lord's grace was truly in the choice of a house on lovely Dewey Lake in Brooklyn, Michigan. Jim and Marilyn can see water from every window in their home. It was Jim's dream come true to be able to walk out their front door and throw a fishing line into the lake.

Marilyn is blessed to be in a parish with an established charismatic prayer group. Two members of the Group also live on Dewey Lake and the three women are close friends. Jim has become active in the local Kiwanis club and Marilyn was invited to join a monthly charitable quilting meeting in the village, widening their circle of friends and acquaintances.

Marilyn thinks the two plaques she put in her yard summarize the miraculous events that led to the move. One reads: "I Will Give You Peace and Quietness," (1 Chronicles 16:11) and the other: "With God All Things are Possible," (Matthew 19:26.) Over the nine years they have lived on Dewey Lake, neighbors tell the couple, "You have the best lot on the lake." Marilyn and Jim surely think so! They thank God daily for their cottage home, and friends and neighbors on Dewey Lake.

In order to hear and discern the Lord's direction in reconciling with her brother, Marilyn sought the help of a Catholic Spiritual director. The wise counsel of this Christian advisor is a special blessing. With her support Marilyn learned many things about herself, as well as new ways to hear God. Her relationship with her brother is improving year after year, with their small family getting together on Dewey Lake for annual family reunions. Marilyn believes she can only ask forgiveness for the things that hurt her brother over the years, especially indirect things that he took to heart. She is also learning patience as she waits for God's timing. Marilyn is confident that as each of them is open to allow God to work, healing will take place between them.

When Jim came home that day and announced to Marilyn that he had lost his job, neither of them had any idea how blessed they would be, as they allowed God to lead in a new direction.

Views of the Troskas' lake home. Water can be seen from every window.

"I AM FORGIVEN!"

Joe Hudy

The clock on the institutional grey wall of Joe Hudy's room in the psychiatric ward read 1:00 am. The sterile sheets pulled tight beneath him, Joe lay on top of the hospital bed, waiting for medication to take effect. The routine was familiar to him. This was the third time in fifteen years Joe had been admitted to the hospital with symptoms of severe depression. In many of life's struggles, Joe's belief in God comforted and sustained him. However, once again, medication seemed the only way to find relief from feelings of loneliness and despair.

In recent years life seemed especially burdensome to him. The old Polish neighborhood where he lived was changing. His home had been burglarized and his cars stolen. The violence around them made his family fear for their safety.

When his mother died, Joe and his wife decided to move the family. Forced by his job as a police officer to maintain residency in Detroit, Joe rented a cramped attic apartment, only able to visit his wife on weekends. He felt like Anne Frank as he looked out of the tiny window to a dreary alley—isolated, missing his family, grieving his mother's death, and witnessing the disintegration of his cherished

66

community. These scenes moved through his mind in the hospital. Suddenly an accusing thought pierced his consciousness, making it difficult for him to breathe.

"You committed one of the seven deadly sins, the sin of anger— because of this sin, you will never see God." The condemning thought pierced his heart.

Joe knew the words were from Satan. He reminded himself that, as a practicing Catholic, if he did his best for God, he believed he would go to heaven. However, instinctively he realized he was not ready to meet the Lord. In fact, Joe had to admit the accusation was true: He *was* angry.

He grew up furious at the severity of his father's discipline. Joe recognized that his father loved the family because of the many kind acts he performed. Nevertheless, Joe was frustrated. He could never tell his father that some of the things he did were wrong, things complicated by a drinking problem. Joe loved his father but he was still angry.

Joe was also angry that he could never seem to measure up to expectations he had been taught as a child. Raised by devout parents, who went to daily Mass, and nurtured in his faith by a Catholic education, he remembered being impressed by the scriptural injunction, "Be perfect as your Father in heaven is perfect," and the warning of a well-meaning nun, "Your soul must be in a perfect state of grace in order to receive communion." Joe knew he was not perfect but he certainly *wanted* to please God. He and his wife and four children were active in their neighborhood parish. His wife had even started a sports program. As Joe fought off the oppression, he cried out to God in desperation, "I am doing all this stuff for you! Why are you allowing this to happen again?"

Now confronted with the truth of the accusation, *"You have committed the sin of anger"* and the resulting judgement, *"and because of this sin you will never see God,"* Joe felt himself slipping into a hopeless pit of darkness. The hospital room became greyer and greyer.

"Is this what it is like to die?' he asked himself."

He was trying to hold onto his essence—his soul—by his fingernails. He imagined if he blinked he would be gone from this life. That is when he heard an audible voice.

"Jesus Christ died on the cross for your sins. Forgive yourself!"

"*That's right!*" Joe shouted into the solitude of his room. Suddenly, the love, the peace, and the joy of the Lord flooded his soul. He knew he was not going to die. God not only loved him, but He had a plan for his life—although at that moment Joe had no idea what that might be.

He looked again at the clock and it was 5:00 am. What had seemed like twenty minutes had actually been four hours.

Joe remained in the hospital for another three weeks. Believing that God's forgiveness and love had instantaneously freed him from guilt and miraculously cured him, he persuaded the psychiatrist to gradually wean him from all medication.

Now God began to give Joe insights into how to live his new life. The first lesson came from his mother-in-law. "Joe, you have to *let go and let God.*" That phrase stays with him even today.

Reading the Bible and listening to Christian radio and television gave him valuable instruction. One day while surfing the channels, he heard a television evangelist promise four keys to cure depression. That captured Joe's attention! The speaker counseled four steps of faith.

1. *Forgive yourself.* This was the cornerstone of Joe's healing experience. "People don't think they are worthy of God's love," Joe elaborated, "If you read scripture, Jesus said, 'I come not to call *the righteous but sinners.*' (Matt. 9:13 NIV) If you don't forgive yourself, what you inadvertently do is make yourself greater than God. When you forgive yourself, God's grace comes to you and you see life in a different way."

2. *Acknowledge God's plan.* Joe pointed out that there are approximately four and a half billion people on the earth and God has a unique plan for each one of them; each individual is special and unique in God's eyes. After twenty-five years as a police officer, observing people at their worst, Joe admitted it has been difficult to see goodness in people. However, asking the aid of the Holy Spirit, he is awed to be able to see others from Christ's point of view.

3. *Allow God the prerogative to direct your life.* Joe explained that with free will, God allows us to make decisions. When we choose to allow God to direct our lives, many blessings follow.

4. *Use the many gifts, blessings, and talents God has poured into your life to help and bless others, and all for God's glory.* Joe has found great satisfaction in taking leadership in groups which allow him to tell his story, express his renewed faith in God, and pass on what he has learned as a follower of Jesus Christ.

The final foundation stone of Joe's newfound confidence was in Jesus' words in Matthew 6:25 and again in Luke 12:21, where Jesus confirms what nature teaches us. God is able and willing to take care of our needs. Joe described these two scriptures as cement that held everything together. With wonder he recounted, "I don't worry about anything. When I start to worry, I just say to myself, 'Let God take care of it.'"

With insight into his struggles Joe recorded in his journal:

"Through the pain you are suffering Christ is purifying you to get rid of your old self and preparing you to put on a new you. It is in your deepest pain, when you feel that you can't go on anymore, that you turn inward to God; let go of your carnal self; and surrender your will to Him. And like the potter molds the clay, so too God is going to *mold your life into what he wants your life to be. Don't give up. He will be there for you.*"